SCIENCE EXPLORER

PONDERING POLLUTION

Follow the Clues

by Tamra B. Orr

CHERRY LAKE PUBLISHING · ANN ARBOR, MICHIGAN

CHERRY LAKE Publishing

Published in the United States of America by Cherry Lake Publishing
Ann Arbor, Michigan
www.cherrylakepublishing.com

CONTENT EDITOR: Melissa Miller, Next Generation Science Standards Writer, Science Teacher, Farmington, Arkansas
BOOK DESIGN AND ILLUSTRATION: The Design Lab
READING ADVISER: Marla Conn, ReadAbility, Inc.

PHOTO CREDITS: Cover and page 1, ©Ungnoi Lookjeab/Shutterstock, Inc.; page 4, ©M. Dykstra/Shutterstock, Inc.; page 5, ©Hurst Photo/Shutterstock, Inc.; page 6, ©3841128876/Shutterstock, Inc.; page 7, ©Boltenkoff/Shutterstock, Inc.; page 8, ©IrinaK/Shutterstock, Inc.; page 9, ©IvicaNS/Shutterstock, Inc.; page 10, ©kontur-vid/Shutterstock, Inc.; page 11, ©bikeriderlondon/Shutterstock, Inc.; page 12, ©Nonwarit/Shutterstock, Inc.; page 13, ©Wendy Kaveney Photography/ Shutterstock, Inc.; page 14, ©Alice Day/Shutterstock, Inc.; page 15, ©Ulrich Mueller/Shutterstock, Inc.; page 16, ©Bart Everett/Shutterstock, Inc.; page 17, ©Leonard Zhukovsky/Shutterstock, Inc.; page 18, ©ssuaphotos/Shutterstock, Inc.; page 19, ©leonello calvetti/Shutterstock, Inc.; page 20, ©Africa Studio/Shutterstock, Inc.; pages 21, 24, and 26, ©Monkey Business Images/Shutterstock, Inc.; page 22, ©Masson/Shutterstock, Inc.; page 23, ©Tooykrub/Shutterstock, Inc.; page 27, ©Sylvie Bouchard/Shutterstock, Inc.; page 28, ©Joe Belanger/Shutterstock, Inc.; page 29, ©sakkmesterke/Shutterstock, Inc.

LIBRARY OF CONGRESS CATALOGING-IN-PUBLICATION DATA
Orr, Tamra, author.
  Pondering pollution / by Tamra B. Orr.
    pages cm. — (Science explorer) (Follow the clues)
  Summary: "Follow along with Sophia as she learns about pollution using the Next Generation Science Standards."— Provided by publisher.
  Audience: Grades 4 to 6.
  Includes bibliographical references and index.
  ISBN 978-1-62431-779-8 (lib. bdg.) — ISBN 978-1-62431-789-7 (pbk.) — ISBN 978-1-62431-809-2 (ebook) — ISBN 978-1-62431-799-6 (pdf)
  1. Air—Pollution—Juvenile literature. 2. Combustion gases—Juvenile literature. 3. Buses—Motors—Exhaust gas—Juvenile literature. I. Title.

TD883.13.O77 2014
363.739'2—dc23   2013038032

Cherry Lake Publishing would like to acknowledge the work of The Partnership for 21st Century Skills. Please visit www.p21.org for more information.

Printed in the United States of America, Corporate Graphics Inc.
January 2014

This book is intended to introduce readers to the Next Generation Science Standards (NGSS). These standards emphasize a general set of eight practices for scientific investigation, rather than a rigid set of steps. Keywords taken from the NGSS are highlighted in the text. The eight science practices are:

1. Asking questions
2. Developing and using models
3. Planning and carrying out investigations
4. Analyzing and interpreting data
5. Using mathematics and computational thinking
6. Constructing explanations
7. Engaging in argument from evidence
8. Obtaining, evaluating, and communicating information

TABLE OF CONTENTS

CHAPTER 1

STRUGGLING TO BREATHE

People with a condition called asthma sometimes need to use an inhaler to help them breathe.

Sophia heard the labored, wheezing sound behind her. She immediately knew what was happening.

"Therese, did you leave your inhaler in your locker again?" Therese nodded, looking embarrassed even as she tried to draw a deep breath. Sophia raced inside the school, running straight to Therese's locker. The girls had been best friends for two years and had memorized each other's locker combinations long ago. Sophia grabbed the inhaler and ran back to the parking lot.

"Here," she said, tossing it to her friend. Therese held the inhaler up to her mouth and took a deep breath. The wheezing gradually began to fade.

Just then, a large yellow school bus pulled up. The side doors slid open, and the girls were last in line to get on. As they neared the bus steps, Sophia gave the driver a concerned look. "Everything okay?" asked the woman behind the wheel.

"We're fine, Mom," replied Sophia. "Therese needed her inhaler, but she is better now." The girls picked up their backpacks and climbed onto the bus.

Sophia and Therese went to the back of the line to board the bus as Therese's medicine started working.

"I'm a little worried about Therese," said Mrs. Alvarez. "Her asthma always seems to act up after school. Are you guys under a lot of stress in class?"

"No more than usual," said Therese, sitting in a seat near the front. Sophia sat down beside her. "I've also had some trouble in the morning."

"What could be making your asthma act up in the morning and afternoon?" Sophia asked.

"That," said Mrs. Alvarez, "is a very good question—and one I think you should explore."

Therese stayed at Sophia's house for a little while so they could discuss Therese's asthma. By the time Mrs. Alvarez finished her bus

Therese and Sophia got off the bus together at Sophia's house.

As a scientist, it is important to keep good records of data.

route and got home, the girls were waiting at the front door. "Therese and I have been talking about her asthma," said Sophia. "We came up with a plan."

Mrs. Alvarez smiled. "Tell me all about it," she said as the three of them sat down in the living room.

"Well, we'll start by keeping track of the times I have trouble with my asthma," explained Therese. "I'll fill out a chart with the time and location each time I need my inhaler."

"We'll also write down what Therese had been doing just before her asthma acted up," added Sophia.

↑ For some people, certain activities can trigger an asthma attack.

"And then we'll look for patterns," finished Therese.

"That sounds like a great plan," said Mrs. Alvarez. "When will you begin your investigation?"

"Sophia and I just finished making the chart. We can start filling it out the next time I need my inhaler," Therese said. "I can't wait to see what we find out!"

TAKE A DEEP BREATH

Scientists begin with a question. This question kicks off an investigation. More often than not, an answer to one question leads to more questions. For example, a scientist might ask, "What happens during an asthma attack?" He or she observes people with asthma and collects data. The scientist determines that **airways** swell and tighten during an asthma attack, which makes it difficult for the person to breathe. This leads to another question: "Why does this swelling occur?" This leads to another investigation, which will lead to more questions and more investigations.

Scientists are still asking questions about asthma. As we learn more about the disease, researchers look for new and better treatments. They study what chemicals can quickly and safely open up airways during an attack. Researchers also look for ways to help prevent an attack from happening.

CHAPTER 2

INVESTIGATING THE PROBLEM

Therese had decided to keep an inhaler in her backpack at all times.

Therese's asthma acted up again two days later. She and Sophia had just sat down on the bus after school.

"Do you have your inhaler?" asked Mrs. Alvarez as the other students climbed onto the bus.

Therese nodded, digging through her backpack. She pulled her inhaler out of the bag's front pouch and brought it to her mouth. She waited until the medicine started working and she could breathe more easily. Then she pulled out the blank chart that she and Sophia had created.

"Thanks," she said as Sophia handed her a pencil.

Therese started filling in the boxes on the chart. "The time is 3:10," she said, looking at her watch. "I was sitting on the bus when it happened, and we had just been waiting for the bus. How long did we stand outside the school before the bus came?"

"About 15 minutes," Sophia answered. Therese wrote this down. The bus started moving, and Therese put the chart back into her bag.

The friends did the same thing each time Therese used her inhaler. Three weeks later, Therese came over to Sophia's house after school to

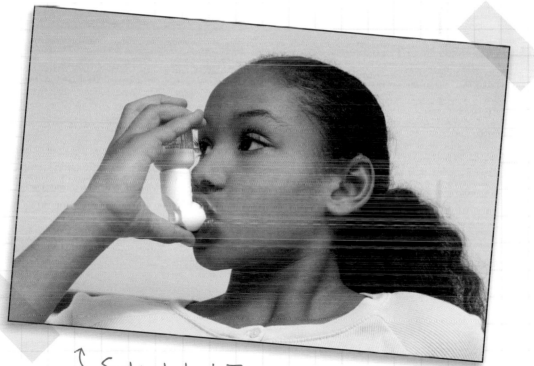

Sophia helped Therese keep track of each time she used her inhaler.

analyze the data they had collected. To help find patterns, the girls decided to create some diagrams. They started by using math, adding up how many times Therese had used her inhaler at each location mentioned on the chart. They also added up the times she used her inhaler after each activity listed. Therese and Sophia turned this information into two bar graphs: one of locations and one of activities. They also printed out a map of their town and marked each place Therese had used her inhaler.

By the time the girls had finished, it was six o'clock. "Well," said Sophia with a sigh, "let's take a break. We can eat dinner and come back to this tomorrow."

"Sounds like a plan," said Therese. "I'm starving!"

Graphs and charts help researchers find patterns in data.

TURNING NUMBERS INTO ANSWERS

Veterinarians can develop asthma from working with animals.

When analyzing data, scientists look for patterns and relationships. South African doctor Jack Pepys researched allergies for much of the 20th century. In his studies, he noticed a pattern in some adults who suffered from asthma. The disease showed up more often in people whose jobs exposed them to a lot of chemicals or other **particulates** in the air, such as woodworkers and metalworkers. Could there be a relationship between occupation and asthma?

The answer is yes. Pepys's analysis revealed that regular exposure to irritating or harmful particulates could cause asthma in workers. The study led to changes not only in workplace safety, but also in our understanding of how asthma can be triggered.

CHAPTER 3

MAKING CONNECTIONS

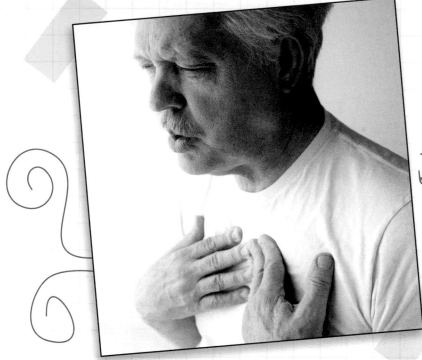

Asthma can make it very difficult for a person to breathe.

"I did some research," said Sophia the next day. She and Therese had just gotten off the bus at Sophia's house and come inside to the living room.

"I did, too," said Therese. "I talked to my Uncle Jack, who is a doctor. He explained what happens during an asthma attack. He even helped me draw a diagram of a person's **respiratory** system to show me how it works." She pulled a piece of paper out of her backpack with the diagram drawn on it. "During an attack, the lungs' airways become swollen, tight, and narrow." Therese pointed to the airways on her diagram. "This

makes it very difficult to take a deep breath. It also makes it much harder to get the oxygen that the body needs to work properly."

"That sounds awfully scary," said Sophia, taking a deep breath of her own.

"It can be," responded Therese. "But there are medicines, such as the medicine in my inhaler, that help open up the airways." Therese set her diagram down. "What did you find?"

"I think I came up with an explanation for your asthma attacks." Sophia picked up a notebook from the coffee table. "I noticed that you use your inhaler most often after riding on the bus or waiting in the parking lot after school. Have you ever noticed how many cars are in the school parking lot in the morning and afternoon?"

Lots of cars and buses go in and out of a school parking lot each day.

"There are a lot of them," said Therese. She thought for a moment and then asked, "Could the cars be triggering my issues with asthma?"

"I think so," said Sophia. "The bus can make your asthma worse, too. My mom helped me find information about car and bus **exhaust** online. I took notes on what we found. It turns out scientists have studied how exhaust and other **pollutants** affect asthma.

"Particulates in the air, such as those found in **soot**, wood smoke, and vehicle exhaust, can be harmful to everyone. But they are especially dangerous to people with asthma or other respiratory problems. The particulates irritate a person's airways and can cause an asthma attack," Sophia explained.

Vehicles produce exhaust, which contains tiny particles that can enter and irritate airways.

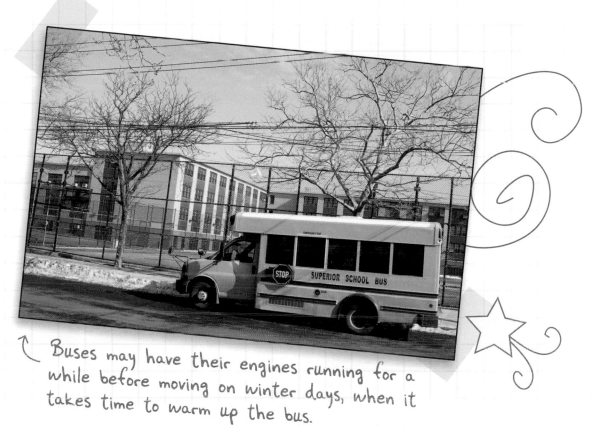

Buses may have their engines running for a while before moving on winter days, when it takes time to warm up the bus.

"The author of one article stated that while buses are on their routes, the exhaust tends to come inside the bus. It's called self-pollution," Sophia went on. "If the windows are closed, the levels of exhaust inside the bus can be up to four times the amount in other vehicles."

"No wonder I have trouble breathing!" exclaimed Therese. "We spend around 30 minutes on the bus each way every day." She made some calculations in Sophia's notebook. "That's about 180 hours spent on the bus each school year."

"Other students spend even longer on the bus," Sophia pointed out. "My cousin Trish rides around an hour and a half each day."

"That's a lot of time to spend around exhaust," said Therese. She looked worried. "There must be some way to cut that time down."

A vehicle produces exhaust whenever its engine is running.

"I did find a possible solution. The Environmental Protection Agency has something called an **Idle** Free Schools campaign. The idea is to draw attention to the pollution that comes from cars and buses that are idling in the parking lots of schools. There's a toolkit that has sample letters, fliers, and charts. Look," Sophia said, pointing to some papers she had printed out the night before. "These are forms you can use to take an idling **survey** at school. You use it to determine how many cars and buses are idling during the week and how much time they spend doing it. That helps you plan what to do about it."

Therese smiled. "I think it's time you and I talk to Principal Lawson. We may have a school project to suggest!"

SEEING IS UNDERSTANDING

Some concepts can be difficult to understand without seeing them in action. Sometimes you can witness an activity or idea in person, such as a sports game or a cooking technique. Other concepts are harder to see, such as processes that take place inside the human body. This is where models come in. A model can be a drawn diagram, a computer animation, or a physical copy. Students studying medicine might use models to learn the parts of the body or understand how certain organs act and interact. A model can also help a patient understand his or her illness.

CHAPTER 4

WORKING ON SOLUTIONS

Sophia and Therese were prepared, bringing plenty of information for Principal Lawson.

"Come in, girls," said Principal Lawson, showing the girls into his office.

"Have you heard about the Environmental Protection Agency's Idle Free Schools campaign?" Sophia asked.

"I've heard of it," replied Principal Lawson. "It's a wonderful program. Do you think our school's air quality is bad enough to need an Idle Free project?"

"We do," said Therese. She and Sophia pulled their charts, graphs, map, and research out of their bags. "The exhaust in the school's parking lot before and after school has been bothering me. Here's the evidence we found to support the idea."

For the next hour, Sophia, Therese, and Principal Lawson discussed the school's air quality.

"Your argument is very convincing," he said. "Let's start this program and gather some more information about idling at our school." He gave Sophia and Therese permission to conduct a survey of the parking lot's levels of **emissions**. He also encouraged the girls to involve as many students as possible. "Invite them to help you do a **baseline** survey," he said. "After we complete it, we can start sharing information about idling with everyone at school."

Sophia and Therese wanted to involve as many other students as possible.

By the end of the week, Sophia and Therese had convinced some of their classmates to help with the survey. Teams were assigned to watch the parking lot and carpool lanes and to correctly fill out the idling charts. A new team was used each day of the week for two weeks.

"You are only to record the information, not influence it," reminded Sophia. "You cannot ask the drivers of cars or buses to turn off their engines. Don't even talk about the program to the drivers because it might change their behavior before we want it to. We need to know exactly how much idling takes place in our parking lot before making any changes."

"I can't wait to see what the idle survey results are!" exclaimed Sophia. "Who knew numbers could be this fascinating?"

↑ Surveyors must collect data carefully and accurately.

Much like a detective, scientists must back up their conclusions with plenty of evidence. In part, evidence helps a scientist make sure his or her conclusion is accurate. Evidence also helps convince other scientists—and the public—that a conclusion is correct. It may take years, multiple investigations, and several scientists to prove that a new idea is correct.

In recent years, scientists have been studying the connection between pollution and asthma. Researchers have found evidence that air pollution makes a person's existing asthma worse and can trigger an attack. Statistics have also shown that a growing number of people are developing asthma in cities, where there is a lot of vehicle traffic and **industrial** activity. Some scientists use this evidence to argue that pollution can cause asthma to develop in someone who never had it before. Research is ongoing, and scientists are finding new evidence all the time.

CHAPTER 5

SHARING INFORMATION AND LOOKING AHEAD

Writing a letter is a way to let members of Congress and other elected officials know what your community needs.

"I'm not surprised you've been having trouble breathing, Therese," said Principal Lawson. He looked at the idling charts. "According to your data, almost three-quarters of the cars and half of the buses idled for 10 minutes or more. The air is full of particulates."

"It looks like it is time to share our findings," said Sophia.

Principal Lawson nodded. "We should involve the whole school. Everyone can help make and put up signs, write letters, and do classroom experiments," he said. "Art classes can work on a **logo**, and the drama group might create a show explaining why vehicle exhaust is such a concern. We can run articles about it in the school newspaper."

They named their project End Idle Time, and took the school by storm. Signs were posted reading,

Letters were sent home to the families of each student, and fliers were handed out in the community. Bus drivers were given pledges to sign. The school established a rule about how much time buses were allowed to idle while waiting for students to load and unload.

More activities followed. Science classes created models showing how the respiratory system works and demonstrated the importance of maintaining healthy, open airways. Therese's Uncle Jack came in to speak to students about the dangers of air pollution and how particulates in

Guest speakers can provide expert information on a certain topic.

News of the End Idle Time project quickly spread to other schools.

exhaust can damage lungs. On another occasion, a local mechanic showed how vehicles produce exhaust and how regular **maintenance** can reduce it. He also discussed how buses of the future would probably use alternative fuels to create less exhaust.

The End Idle Time project was a huge success. News of the school's project soon spread, and other schools asked Therese and Sophia to visit and explain how the project works.

"Who knew so much could happen just because I forgot my inhaler?" asked Therese with a grin. She stopped to get a drink from one of the

↑ What do you know about your community's water supply?

school's water fountains. Just as she finished swallowing, she paused and looked thoughtfully at the water trickling down the drain.

"What's wrong?" asked Sophia. "Does it taste funny?"

"I was just wondering how clean our water supply really is . . ." Therese's voice trailed off.

"That," said Sophia, "is a very good question—and one I think we should explore."

AN APP FOR AIR QUALITY

The information scientists learn can affect people around the world, so sharing their findings is important. Organizations such as the Environmental Protection Agency and the World Health Organization share information in a variety of ways. Posters can introduce an idea simply and clearly in a picture or a few words. Brochures and Web sites might explain ideas more thoroughly, using simple language that people who have not studied science might understand.

Some organizations have developed applications for phones and tablet computers. These programs might send users up-to-the-minute data and risk warnings. If you have an iPhone or Android phone, you can keep tabs on your own school's air quality through a State of the Air app. Supported by the American Lung Association, this app checks the air quality where you live on a daily basis. It lets you know if there are days when you should take extra precautions. You can find details at www.lung.org /healthy-air/outdoor/state-of-the-air/app.html.

GLOSSARY

airways (AIR-wayz) the body's pathways for air to flow into the lungs

analyze (AN-uh-lize) to examine something carefully in order to understand it

baseline (BASE-line) a line serving as a basis, as for measurement

emissions (i-MISH-uhnz) substances released into the atmosphere

exhaust (ig-ZAWST) the gas or steam produced by the engine of a motor vehicle

idle (EYE-duhl) for a vehicle's engine to be running without the vehicle being in motion

industrial (in-DUHS-tree-uhl) having to do with factories and making things in large quantities

logo (LOW-go) a distinctive symbol that identifies a particular company or organization

maintenance (MAYN-tuh-nuhns) the process of keeping something in good condition by checking and repairing it

particulates (par-TIK-yuh-luts) extremely small, separate particles or pieces

pollutants (puh-LOO-tuhnts) substances that contaminate another substance

respiratory (REHS-pur-uh-tor-ee) describing the process of breathing in and breathing out

soot (SUT) black powder that is produced when a fuel is burned

survey (SUR-vay) a study of the opinions or behaviors of a group of people

FOR MORE INFORMATION

BOOKS

Feinstein, Stephen. *Solving the Air Pollution Problem: What You Can Do.* Berkeley Heights, N.J.: Enslow Publishers, 2011.

Royston, Angela. *Explaining Asthma.* Mankato, Minn.: Smart Apple Media, 2010.

Sechrist, Darren. *Air Pollution.* Tarrytown, N.Y.: Marshall Cavendish Benchmark, 2009.

Silverstein, Alvin. *Handy Health Guide to Asthma.* Berkeley Heights, N.J.: Enslow Publishers, 2013.

WEB SITES

The Clean Air Campaign

www.cleanaircampaign.org/Your-Schools

Learn more about what you can do to improve the air at your school and in your community.

United States Environmental Protection Agency—Idle Free Schools

www2.epa.gov/region8/idle-free-schools

Use this site to explore the Idle Free Schools Toolkit, and learn about other programs to combat exhaust and particulates.

INDEX

ABOUT THE AUTHOR

Tamra B. Orr is an author living in the Pacific Northwest. Orr has a degree in Secondary Education and English from Ball State University. She is the mother to four, and the author of more than 350 books for readers of all ages. When she isn't writing or reading books, she is writing letters to friends all over the world. Although fascinated by all aspects of science, most of her current survey skills are put to use trying to figure out what everyone wants for dinner and which movie to watch.